DOGS

DACHSHUNDS

by Elizabeth Andrews

Cody Koala
An Imprint of Pop!
popbooksonline.com

Hello! My name is Cody Koala

This book is filled with videos, puzzles, games, and more! Scan the QR codes* while you read, or visit the website below to make this book pop.

popbooksonline.com/dachshund

*Scanning QR codes requires a web-enabled smart device with a QR code reader app and a camera.

abdobooks.com

Published by Pop!, a division of ABDO, PO Box 398166, Minneapolis, Minnesota 55439.

Printed in the United States of America, North Mankato, Minnesota.

102022
012023

THIS BOOK CONTAINS RECYCLED MATERIALS

Cover Photo: Shutterstock Images
Interior Photos: Shutterstock Images
Editor: Grace Hansen
Series Designer: Colleen McLaren

Library of Congress Control Number: 2022941107

Publisher's Cataloging-in-Publication Data

Names: Andrews, Elizabeth, author.
Title: Dachshunds / by Elizabeth Andrews
Description: Minneapolis, Minnesota : Pop!, 2023 | Series: Dogs | Includes online resources and index.
Identifiers: ISBN 9781098243180 (lib. bdg.) | ISBN 9781098243883 (ebook)
Subjects: LCSH: Dachshund--Juvenile literature. | Badger dogs, German--Juvenile literature. | Domestic Dog--Juvenile literature. | Zoology--Juvenile literature.
Classification: DDC 636.753--dc23

Table of Contents

Chapter 1

Badger Hound

The name dachshund (dahks-hund) is made of two German words. *Dachs* means badger. *Hund* means dog. Dachshunds were **bred** in Germany 600 years ago to hunt **burrowing** animals.

Watch a video here!

A dachshund's strong, pointy nose helps it find animals. Its long, low-to-the-ground body allows the dog to fit into small spaces. Though dachshunds are small, they are **hearty** hunters!

Chapter 2

The Look

Dachshunds come in two sizes. The standard size is eight to nine inches (20–23cm) tall and 16 to 32 pounds (7.2–14.5kg). Miniatures are five to six inches (13–15cm) tall and weigh less than 11 pounds (5kg).

Miniature dachshunds were **bred** to hunt rabbits. Standard dachshunds can handle larger animals, such as foxes and badgers.

Learn more here!

longhaired

smooth

wirehaired

Dachshunds can have smooth, longhaired, or wirehaired coats. Their coats come in many colors, like red, black, cream, and tan. The coat can also have different markings.

Wirehaired dachshunds were bred to hunt in thorny plants.

Chapter 3

Personality and Care

Though dachshunds were **bred** to hunt on their own, they love their families. Dachshunds are **stubborn** and smart. Owners need lots of patience during training.

Explore links here!

Hunting dogs have energy and were bred to follow their nose. So, dachshunds can find trouble if left alone

for too long. Leaving them home with toys or another dog is best.

Dachshunds are loving and like to be included in activities. They often choose a favorite family member to claim as their own. They are **loyal** and can play well with children.

Longhaired and wirehaired dachshunds need to be brushed weekly. They also need their ears cleaned and toes clipped regularly. The pups should visit the vet for checkups.

Dachshunds are little dogs who love food. They can quickly become overweight. Their food intake should be **monitored**.

Chapter 4

Puppies

Like all dogs, dachshunds are born deaf and blind. They start hearing and seeing at ten to 14 days old. At eight weeks, the puppies are ready for **adoption**. New owners should start training right away!

Complete an activity here!

Making Connections

Text-to-Self

What is your favorite feature of the dachshund? Explain your answer.

Text-to-Text

Have you read any other books about hunting dogs? What did they have in common with the dachshund?

Text-to-World

The dachshund is from Germany. What are other dogs that have come from different countries?

Glossary

adoption – the act of accepting an animal as a pet and taking on the responsibility of it.

bred – developed to act and look a specific way, or serve a certain purpose.

burrowing – denoting an animal that makes holes or tunnels, often to live in.

hearty – strong and sturdy.

loyal – dedicated to someone or something.

monitor – to watch closely and check on.

stubborn – not willing to accept change, help, or control.

Index

Online Resources

popbooksonline.com

Thanks for reading this Cody Koala book!

This book is filled with videos, puzzles, games, and more! Scan the QR codes* while you read, or visit the website below to make this book pop.

popbooksonline.com/dachshund

*Scanning QR codes requires a web-enabled smart device with a QR code reader app and a camera.